CW00524221

DO NOTHING
ACHIEVE
EVERYTHING

DO NOTHING
ACHIEVE
EVERYTHING

AWAKENING FROM
THE GRAND ILLUSION

by

Michael Mackintosh

DO NOTHING
ACHIEVE EVERYTHING

TO THE ONE,
THE OCEAN OF PEACE

WHAT IF THERE WAS A SECRET TO LIFE THAT FEW PEOPLE EVER TALK ABOUT?

What if there was ONE main cause to all your suffering?

What if freeing yourself from that main cause could liberate you from all the suffering in your life for good?

What if the reason you have negative thoughts, relationship challenges, confusion, money problems or health issues ALL stemmed from this one big thing...

And if you freed yourself it would allow you to enter into beautiful states of peace, love, freedom, lightness and inner joy at will...

Would you be interested in finding out what it was?

Not only does solving this core problem liberate you from countless forms of suffering, it also helps you manifest happiness, peace, wealth, love and power in your life.

Do you want to know what it is?

This book gives you the secret to attain true freedom in life.

But before you discover the secret and apply it - you first have to make a choice.

CHOICE # 1:
THE OLD WAY OF BEING

If you want to feel good and have success in life you can follow the old way that nearly everyone around you is obsessed about.

In the old way you hope that by getting more and more stuff you will finally feel better and have a great life.

It's based on the myth that to live a happy and successful life you have to get good grades, work hard in a job, get married, get the kids, get the house, car and big TV and take vacations.

Then one day you can finally retire and enjoy the good life.

The problem with this is for most people, getting the stuff they think they want is stressful. It hurts them every day. They have to force themselves to get the result they want. And even worse, as soon as they get the thing they wanted (the grades, job, marriage, kids, house etc.) they feel burdened by the next thing they are required to do. Not only did they not get real happiness from the things they wanted, their minds are always worried about losing what they have or not getting the next thing on the list.

In the old way, you put on a show, disrespect yourself and try and fit in with other people. You can work yourself half to death hoping to make tons of money so you can feel powerful and secure. You can do endless diets and exercise programs in the hopes you'll create great health and stay young, healthy and beautiful forever.

But, in the end you have no guarantee anything will work. You have no guarantee you'll be any happier when you get the things you wanted.

And the honest truth is, no matter how hard you worked - one day your body will die and you'll lose it all.

Everything you worked for will all be taken away and all you will be left with is the state of being that you used to create your life.

If you died today you'd be left with your emotional state and your mind.

If that's ALL you had, how rich would you be?

If all you were was a mind and heart, with nothing else, how would you feel?

How much peace, love, bliss, freedom, joy and abundance do you have inside?

How wealthy is your inner kingdom?

The old way often gives so much attention to trying to control the outside world that we are left bankrupt and depressed no matter how hard we try.

The good news is there is another way.

You already know it exists. You've experienced it in peak moments and feel the magic of this other way of being. Now is your chance to embrace it and enjoy it in your life.

CHOICE # 2:
THE ETERNAL WAY

The Eternal way allows you to have all the success you want in life WITHOUT the pain and inner bankruptcy.

It creates wealth, abundance and freedom as by products of feeling good today.

It's the opposite approach to the old way.

It's focused on instant results, not on endless series of disappointments.

The eternal way is so radically different, that it's barely possible to comprehend with your normal mind.

The eternal way is not anti-action. In fact, it embraces action. It embraces making things happen in the 'world'. It includes success in life on the physical level and acknowledges the importance of being responsible, clear and focused on what's important to create a life of health, wealth and happiness.

But it embraces all these things from a radically different place. It's not about striving to do things to feel good later.

It's not about 'have to's and 'should's.

It's about something far deeper and more profound.
And it will radically transform your life forever.

HOW DO YOU BEGIN LIVING THIS ETERNAL WAY?

The eternal way is natural. It's how you'd be living WITHOUT the programming you received from childhood. It's a state of being that is as natural as breathing - and yet it's as rare as waking up one morning and finding your home has been turned into pure gold.

To experience this new state of being you first need to

S L O W   D O W N

And

R E L A X

The fastest way to reach this state is to STOP.

It's the opposite of what we've been taught and it will take you some time to truly 'get' what is going on.

But once you 'wake up' from the trance you've been in - you'll see clearly what the #1 secret is.

You'll wonder how you could ever have forgotten these things. And yet, no words will ever be able to truly describe what it is you are experiencing.

This all may sound abstract and strange to your mind. And frankly, it is. The mind will never truly 'get' what is being said here. You can read all day about the taste of apples. But you will never truly know the taste of an apple until you put one in your mouth and take a bite...

The same is true here.

It's about awakening to that deeper part of you, the REAL you that exists before and after death.

Deep down you already know the person you see in the mirror is not who you are. You know you are so much more than how you look.

You know most people don't 'get' you.

You know one day your body will die.

And along with it, your name, age, sex, titles and all your stuff will be gone. Everything you used to own will no longer be yours to control. You won't be able to talk face to face with your friends and family, nor will you be able to do the things you enjoyed while in a body.

This day can happen to anyone at any time.

But don't worry.

This book is not about sitting around all day doing nothing and hoping your life will improve. It's not a book on 'the Law of Attraction'. It's not about how to manifest a new car, better house or some other physical desire.

What this book is about is remembering WHO YOU ARE before and after death. And returning back to your natural state of being, where you are merged in grace.

From this natural state of being it's quite possible you will manifest and attract all kinds of wonderful things into your life, but that's not what this is about.

This book is simply about being in the eternal Reality that never went anywhere and that no technique can bring into existence. What is Real and Eternal can never change, and is not dependent on you or anyone else doing anything.

This book is about Doing Nothing and Attaining Everything without effort. It's about awakening from the 'Grand Illusion' that you, the Eternal Self, are ever lacking anything.
And returning back to your original state of freedom that you are right now.

This book is about waking up to your vast power and experiencing a state of total peace, freedom and lightness that is always present behind all experiences. It's about tapping back into the Ground of Consciousness that can never be destroyed and allows your experience to emerge right now.

This book can't 'do anything' for you. It's merely a window into what IS. It can't give you anything you don't already have. What this book can do is point you back at the Light you are, and open your heart and mind to what you may have forgotten - but lives inside of you always.

In this book you'll find the 'letters'; moments of inspiration that came to me early in the morning over several years. I put pen to paper and what you read is what emerged, un-edited and direct. It felt like God/Higher Power/Creator/Source was giving me insights and touchings on things that didn't make sense to my mind, but touched my soul.

Many times my conscious mind didn't understand the messages I received. But I felt the truth of them.

Your mind and personality may not understand these messages either. But that doesn't matter.

Because they are direct experiences of non-linear, non-physical states of being and they do not follow normal logical, left-brain structures. They are not written for satisfying your mind. They are for YOU, the soul, to relax into. They are pointers towards something that exists forever.

You may find it helpful to see these passages as meditations to reflect on. As gentle reflections on deeper things that exist behind and beyond the mind.

You can pick any one to read at random. You can read from beginning to end, or end to beginning. It doesn't matter.

Follow your inspiration.

The main thing is to slow down, relax and allow yourSELF to emerge. You ARE what you seek. You CAN attain everything, as an experience inside of you.

Only you can awaken yourSelf - and the more you let go, relax and stop trying, the faster that will occur.

I hope you enjoy these words on That which exists beyond words and beyond the mind.

Much love,

Michael Mackintosh
Kauai, Hawaii

DO NOTHING

FORWARD

I should tell you,

This book would not be published if I hadn't discovered these
sheets of brilliance, hidden away in a crowded cupboard.

Michael Mackintosh, a spiritual teacher of 15 years, had been
'channeling' these jewels of wisdom for years at 4 o'clock in the
morning, but had never thought twice about sharing them with
others.

He had them all tucked away, adding to this pile of golden
insight frequently.

One day, I stumbled upon some of these papers while tidying
up around the house.

I read them and was floored by the level of consciousness
in which they were written. This was not Michael's normal
writing. He is, already, remarkably wise and insightful, with a

depth of spiritual knowledge deeper than most common day gurus. But this, this was something else.

This was some of the deepest and most profound material I'd ever read.

Absorbed in the spiritual intoxication and bliss these writings elicit, I found myself spontaneously entering higher states of consciousness. Snapping out of my normal waking consciousness, and into a field of great depth of knowing, wisdom and peace.

I'd experienced such states during my silent meditation practice, and now having poetic words to go with my experiences awakened a song in my heart.

I knew these needed to be shared and convinced Michael to finally let them be released.

What you hold before you are messages of Truth; higher guidance and direction from the One.

Michael has been connecting with the One; The Supreme Soul/God since he was 18. These letters are a testament to the intimacy and personal relationship each of us can have with the Divine.

If we just open ourselves to receive...

And welcome the divine knowledge and spiritual powers that come through.

Sit back, relax and enjoy a deep journey into the heart and mind of The One; the Ocean of Peace.

For these writings will introduce you to this One.

Om Shanti; Peaceful Vibrations,

Arielle Hecht
Kauai 2014

DO NOTHING

INTRODUCTION

This is not your average self-help book that teaches 'success methods' or how to get things done faster and better.

Nor is it like most books on spirituality and meditation that share techniques and practices that try to help you reduce stress and experience peace.

While those books can be useful stepping stones on our path, there comes a point where 'getting things done better' and reducing stress are no longer as important as they once were. You've moved on. And as your own perception about life evolves, something deeper and more fundamental is needed for you to go to the next level in your evolution.

And that's what you have here. A doorway into a new way of being that solves all problems without force and allows you to be free of pain, struggle, worry, anxiety and drama. But the challenge you will face in what you're about to discover is not obvious, it's counter-intuitive - and it's not a 'how to' step-by-step system you can learn.

In fact, it's both radically simple and yet profoundly complex at the same time and only when you're ready will you begin to embrace this 'open secret' that's always been there - smiling back at you.

TO TAKE THINGS DEEPER...

This book gives you insights into new ways of being. To help you integrate this new state of consciousness, I've included access to the Accession TookKit: A power series of audios, videos, guided meditations and commentaries to explain these insights further and help you accelerate your spiritual evolution.

Access your Ascension TookKit for FREE
at the address below:

attaineverything.com

Enjoy the book.

Remember to go slow and don't worry about your conscious mind understanding everything.
Your heart and soul will ;-).

THE ETERNAL SELF

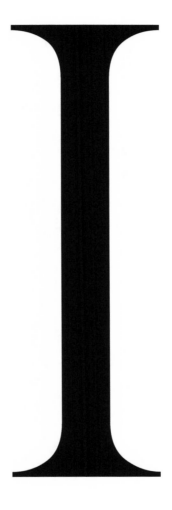

WHAT IS HERE NOW?

You are a soul
This means you are infinite divine light
And eternal peace

What else do you need
But to enjoy this magnificent experience?

What is better than the core
Unlimited and ever present experience
Of what is right now?

Your biggest trap is trying to 'get something done'
Trying so hard to achieve something
That is constantly present

Imagine trying to eat a cake through your thumbs
Rather than your mouth
And getting frustrated
As the cake is crushed and wasted

You already have everything today

You need nothing
But fail to see the truth
Of what is all around you now

Right now
Not some other time
In some distant place
But right here
Right now

Do you get the picture?
Do you want to relax and enjoy the cake?
Or are you too absorbed in twisted pursuits
Of endless distraction?

Only you can answer these questions
And change your eyes to see what is really happening
all the time

Open your eyes now
And you will see

I AM

I am the eternal power I am

Beyond all name and form I am

Free from all thoughts and sensations I am

Outside of time and space I am

Beyond the appearance of 'me' I am

Absolute, eternal, immortal I am

All I see, hear, feel, and experience I am

Beyond and without all that is seen, heard and
experienced I am

No matter what people say or do or don't do I am

Silent and everlasting I am

Light beyond light; form beyond form I am

Sweetness expressed in a smile I am

Smile contained in sweetness I am

Formless, beyond the face and eyes I am

Seeing through the eyes of time I am

Lifted out from both thoughts and opinions I am

With no need to be right or prove a point I am

Outside of time, space and sound I am

Never-ending and un-asking I am

All people die, all familiar scenes end and I am

All dreams vanished, all fears forgotten I am

All problems solved, all needs fulfilled I am

Total dissatisfaction, craving and obsession I am

Total abandonment of all that is wanted or desired I am

Broken bones and broken hearts and tears I am

Illness, sickness, tiredness and worry abound I am

Untainted by all experience of the body, heart and mind I am

Without understanding and comprehension of 'I' I am

Amidst the greatest pleasure and endless pain I am

Throughout all time and ideas of time I am

Never cut, nor burned, nor dried out, nor drowned I am

Eternal peace, love, bliss, power and purity I am forever

I am That I am

I am awake as I awaken I am

In deep sleep, in dream world, in waking I am

Beyond time, space and sound I am

Free of all good and bad opinions of others I am

Included as all imagination, perception and fantasy I am

Unending, everlasting eternal peace and silence I am

Om Shanti - I the soul am an embodiment of peace

My original religion is peace I am

I am

I am

I merge into THAT

IT'S HAPPENING

Stuff is just happening

It's up to us to decide how to interpret it

Essence

Consciousness

Nonlinear and non-dual

Constant, permanent, unlimited, endless

The details of life are various

Changing, limited

They have a start and finish

The ego is based on the details

It's life is all about promoting the details

That make it feel self-important

Real

And avoiding everything that challenges it

Consciousness
Soul
Self

Is the backdrop that all this is experienced upon
It has no need to feel good about the details of the ego

It is
All that is

It is the bliss that the ego is forever missing
But always grasping for

It has attained everything
And needs nothing ever
Because it is constant divine light
And endless peace

There is nothing to be happy about

Happiness

Peace

Contentment

Are already there in the soul

As a constant ground

From which all else has the capacity to arise

The closeness we have to this ground

This field of truth

Reality

Consciousness that we are

The more happiness, freedom, grace and love

We naturally experience

Regardless of what circumstances

May or may not be occurring

In the drama

No matter what details emerge

The field of consciousness

That holds everything

Is permanent and endless

This spiritual work

Is to disassociate the sense of 'I' 'me' 'self' 'my'
With anything in the manifest domain

And relax back into the constant backdrop
Of the soul
The infinite divine light

The closer we are to this
The more grace
Constantly fills our experience of life

Attempting to manifest
On the basis of the ego wanting stuff to feel good
Is fraught with obvious problems
And guarantees failure
Because it is not the stuff
That can bring true satisfaction

Allowing and surrendering to the Source
Gives us an experience of infinite divine love
That can only attract to itself the same as it is

Upgrade your level of consciousness

EVERYTHING AND NOTHING

Breathe in

Breathe out

Time lets go as you fly

Hold onto nothing

And become everything

Attain everything

Remember

You've already attained it all

Behind your mind

Below the emotional ways

Under your heavy heart

And self-centered burdens

You'll find silence

Bliss

An ever present peace

Breathe in

Breathe out

Time lets go and you fly away

Hold on to nothing Fear and Nothing

FEAR AND NOTHING

All fear comes from loss

The more you have

The more you have to lose

The more you need

The less you smile

Your fear owns you

Your stuff controls you

Your mind outsmarts you

And cages your soul

In an invisible box

You call

"My life"

Are you willing to die alive?

Die to all you are and all you own?

Death to your dreams

Death to your needs and wants and visions?

Can you move away?
Can you let go?
Can you die and breathe in peace?
Nothing is freedom
Nothing is freedom

Your whole world is imaginary
How deluded you are to be afraid
Of fictional fragments in your mind
Scared of pretend people
And cartoon characters

You created them all
And now you are afraid
They will attack and scare you away?

Your mind is imaginary
Your mind holds all the keys
Why do you let yourself get so lost?

Are you ready to awaken from this trance

And smile

And be

Free?

Who would you be without struggle

And fear and drama and sadness?

What would be left if you didn't care

And stopped waiting till later to smile?

How many saddened moments do you need

Before you finally let go?

Do it today and let your life speak for itself

Die and be reborn right now

NOT ME

All you can see
Is "not me"

The mirror spins webs of lies
In time

And as you awaken
And recognize

Your life makes sense
And all that's done
Fades away
Drifts into the distance
Falls into insignificance

You're not what you see

You're not what you can hear

Nothing is left except the smiling star

The light that beams away eternally
At the back of the room in your mind

Let all emotions come to you
And be alone as One

Just you
In the silence of the night
Awake at last

AWAKEN

Awaken

You have been sleeping deeply

Nothing can stir a sleeping Angel

Who is unwilling to let go of the old

Your call is loud and profound

Can you hear it?

Or are you pretending the world doesn't suffer?

People are terrified

They can't sleep

Can you hear it?

Or are you still unable to get out of bed your self?

Awaken and breathe in divine light

Drink in pure love and soul nectar

Open your heart and soul to me

And as I pour onto you let it spill over

Into the hearts of your family

May they be happy and forever full
Do you realize who you are and why you are here?
Embrace your light and love thyself
Awake and sail across the seas of slumber
Discover the hidden horizons of your soul
Your life is boring without this
You will never satisfy your cravings for rest
Until you awaken and rest in my lap
In the arms of true love and bliss

These are not words

This is your birthright
It is all around you now
Are you awake to feel it?
Are you here now?
Stay awake tonight
And experience life for yourself

THE LIGHT OF THE SOUL

THE LIGHT OF THE SOUL
CAN SEE NO LIGHT
IT IS THE LIGHT

THE GRAND ILLUSION

All you see

All you perceive

On all levels of your life

Is all fake

A grand illusion

Springs a web in time

No face nor place

Initiation or ending

Will hold on forever

Falling through the net

Your movements crash

Upon the lakes of time

Shimmering light, glistening

A chorus of eternity

STOP and stand here

Step back and allow

Really step back and allow
Really step back and allow

And you'll see
The shimmering waters will dry up
And nothing you knew will remain

A dry lake, cracked earth
No trace of life
No trace of time
And yet here you are

Ablaze with power
Alight with the force of forever

Let the puppets play in the lake
And let your mind rest in calm cold

Let it fall
Let it fall
Let it fall

Catch nothing and you will
Find no fear
Let it fall

THE SEEKER

I've gone as far as I can on my own

I'm tired and plagued with wasteful thoughts and desires

Come into my mind and heart and my life

And show me grace

Tell me the secrets I can't see

And guide me as I pass through the valley of the shadow of death

You keep Me far away

You are asking for help, but you don't mean it

Your heart deceives you

And your mind blinds you

Are you truly ready for instruction?

Or are you just desperate and seeking solace?

By now I've lost myself in distractions and pleasures of comfort

I've created a kingdom that pleases me

But hurts my heart and soul with the lack of true love

I'm missing the beauty of spiritual bliss I've tasted

And feel dried up and depressed

Not always -

But when I awaken in the morning
Too often my heart is filled with regret

I know I am distant from your presence
And I know it's available but I lack the power to take it

My desires and tiredness pull me under
I act impulsively
I need help
I'm asking because I'm ready to be taught
I'm teachable. I'm willing to make sacrifices and face ordeals.
I want the hero's path.
Teach me.

Your days are wasted in thinking and doing

You think you're clever but in truth you are a fool

A ship of fools that rattles away at nothing

True innovation comes from silence and you have none

You may sit down quietly, but your mind races and shifts and
screams

You lack discipline and the heart to apply it

Are you sure you are truly ready to learn the deepest secrets and
use them?

Why?

I agree, my mind is full of nonsense

My heart is addicted to pleasures and my eyes deceive me

My dreams are far from pure and I'm tired

I'm ready because I'm afraid I'll get worse

And my life will collapse slowly but surely

Without your power

I know I'm missing the power and the grace to achieve my dreams

I've reached my limit and I'm humble

I'll set up extremely clear and hard-core accountability to make sure

I do what you say

Teach me

There are only two things for you to learn and know

They are one and the same but start from different corners

of your life

The first is your actions

What you do each day burns a stain into your mind

Call it a pattern, a habit, a force if you like

It goes in and runs itself

Nearly all you do is unconscious and you have no control

over it

That's why paying attention to your daily rituals and habits is
essential

They end up owning it

You didn't just drink coffee or watch movies once

You grind the habit in

And soon it happens without your wish

Nothing can ever stop the power of a fully formed habit

Except Divine Grace and surrender

Or you come back to these habits later

Surrender is the real key to change

You must be willing to let go of everything and die

You must be open to your own death and rebirth

You must accept the pain of death too

Not just to die, but to cry and die

The greater your surrender

The greater the power of new life is formed

Jump off the cliff into the abyss

Give your mind to Me

Not as a nice idea

But as a tangible reality

Are you willing to die?

Yes and no

Part of me is ready

And if I'm honest another part has heard it all before

And may agree but will resist and do nothing

What can I do?

Death means death

There are no half deaths here

To surrender a flower into the fire means

To let the flower go

Release it from your control

And surrender it to the will of the flames

Are you willing to do that for your mind?

Your money?

Your clothes, your contacts and connections?

Your food? Your business and service? Your ideas?

Imagine taking all you have and releasing it into the fire of peace

Can you do this?
Are you willing to do it?

Will you run and hide
Or ignore me and walk away?

No I'm ready.
I'm trying to run away
But there is nowhere left to go

Then do nothing
Be nothing - except a point of peace in an eternal sky
Fall deep into this eternal sky where nothing else remains
Until you can do this first step
You are not ready for me
Become a point of peace and dance silently in the
immortal sky

Surrender it all up from
Your soul
If you like, you can breathe in my peace
Hold it as a point of peace

I

What we say is 'I'

Is just

An accumulation

Of what has simply

"Happened" to a

Character in a movie

Just because 'Tom' went for a walk

Or he ate a pie...

Since when does it mean

'I' went for a walk

'I' ate a pie?

Consciousness is unlimited and nonphysical

It doesn't have a pair of human legs to walk anywhere

And has nowhere to go

It has no need to eat pie

Or a mouth to use

Stay here in a place of limitless freedom

And you are safe to be "me"

Drop back to truth

And stay in the comfort

Of eternal peace

And eternal bliss

Jeevan Mukti

THE COMBINED FORM

I am That I am

I never allow you to learn

Without suffering

So you truly learn

What is the law of life

You are on the right track

The happiness track

You are doing great

Aim

For the

Constant Combined form

Constant endlessly, forever

Combined with Me

Not that you stay in expansion

But you are combined

You are eternally connected

Forever

Together as one Being

This is what makes all the difference

Combined together

Glued as one

Never separated

No individual self

The Combined Self

Being combined is where

The real joy comes from

The real magic of life

The wonder of life

It transforms all

It brings you into the end

At the beginning

And all things will be

Revealed to you in time

It is done

It is done

It Is done

Thank you, thank you

Consider it done NOW

Feel the end result

Without fear or questions

There is nothing left

It is all done

Finally complete

The end

The end

Thank you

UNCHANGING

I feel depressed, needy, unsatisfied, dehydrated, uninspired,
lazy and bored

Who you are
And how you feel
Are not the same

You are what you are originally and eternally

No feeling can ever change that
No matter how strong it is
Realize this and awaken

If you feel low, tired, needy, depressed, sad, grey - relax
This is a passing cloud
Breathe
Breathe some more
Focus your attention on the seat of the soul
Shining star between and behind your eyes
Know you sit here in complete majesty and power

You do well here in infinite peace

Stop and look at yourself

You have forgotten who you are

And where you reside

Stop

Breathe and take note

Of the facts of your own existence

You are eternal light

Talk to yourself

"I am eternal light

I am an immortal spiritual light

I am a witness of this body; this scene

I am an embodiment of peace"

Stop and do this for a while

Lie and rest by the ocean

Or in nature if you so choose

When you awaken

Simply say

L I

F E

YOU CALL THIS LIFE

Time will tell the course of your inner life

As it spews up from the corners of your soul

Into the manifest world

Nothing will ever and can ever remain hidden

Relax now in the knowing

All is exactly as it is planned to be at this time

This moment

All details are perfectly organized

To reflect your deeper yearnings,

Attitudes, ideas, perceptions, confusions and knowingness

Without the outer reflection of your world

It would be hard for you to see your own mind

And the inner workings of your soul

Sit for a moment and ponder this

Look about you and see your inner state

As reflected back at you

Through an unlimited fabric

Of objects, colors, people, systems, vibrations

Gaze and ponder this wonder

Recognize your creation

What do you see?

How do you feel?

From where inside of you did this emerge?

Rest assured that all you perceive

Is recorded inside your soul

Inside yourself

Your experience of life would simply not exist

If it did not first exist in the un-manifest realm

You are in fact a walking movie reel

You are spontaneously and automatically producing
movements,

changes, moments in an endless stream of multi-dimentional

experience

You call this life

You see it as time and space

But from where did the past arise?

From where will the future arise?

Breathe and watch this spontaneous outflow

Of movement in time

It is happening all of its own accord

Watch it

Enjoy it for a while now

Stop

Wait and wonder

Look how you seem to own and dis-own various parts of

your experience

If you wake up - you will see all of it as a passing cloud

Not any sense of 'I'

There will be no consciousness of doing anything or being

anything

Look

Everything you see, feel, hear, taste, sense, smell, touch

Is all made of dream stuff

The person you appear to be

Will one day fade away

And even the memory will cloud over

And vanish

Just as you have experienced

With previous incarnations

Do you recall your last five lives?

Do you feel 'I am so and so from this place' anymore?

Not likely

You don't even remember what was your central

And un-relentless obsession for a whole lifetime, do you?

That previous person is long gone

And barely even a trace of it exists now

Consider your current incarnation as just the same

You are not the name, age, sex, role you see and feel yourself

to be

You are the same one who watched

As the others came and went

You were the witness then in those lives

And you are the witness still now

Right now

So then, choose your course of action

What do you want?

Do you want to be obsessed

And lost in a dream player?

Or do you want to awaken

And smile upon your world a golden smile of love and light?

Would you choose freedom or slavery?

Darkness and compression

Or divine light and unlimited wonder?

Take the time to ponder, contemplate,

And absorb this choice

And awaken

You are not who you appear to be

That image will disappear

And you will be left with your Self

Again

You'll discover you are

And always were,

NOTHING IS WHAT IT SEEMS

I feel weird. Guilty. Dreadful. Excited and angry.

What to do? How can I truly surrender myself to you?

What's really going on? Tell me. I'm anxious.

Dear one,

Nothing is what it seems

Deeper down lies deeper treasures

All guilt and shame is ego made

To run is not to free yourself

To be free

Is to be in life

With power

You are deeper down

You are the world you see

And it's in you

Running away from yourself

Or your life

Solves nothing

You are only running away from nothing

And then running away from nothing again

What is true substance is always true

It's always powerful

Align with That

Lust, ego, attachment, greed will all love to eat you

Stand strong

Go deep and find the ONE

If you are happy

For all your communication

To be presented before me

You are free

Start now

Let everything be open

And breathe deep

Become a point of light

Stay a point

LIVE EACH DAY AS

You're doing too much for too little

Do less of something great

Be the example

Don't get trapped

Be it

Live each day as if it was your last

People are watching you

Share the truth

Be that

Let go of the loss

Focus on the gain

IF IT WAS YOUR LAST

Choose your cards wisely

Leave aside all you want

And be all you are

BIG
CLEAR
POWERFUL
BEAUTIFUL

PRIORITIZE BLISS

Your life is a precious gift

Use it wisely

Allow for the pause

Between the breath

Sit for a moment

And dwell upon your inner smile

Then act

To stop

And reveal the incognito power

That is driving everything in existence

Means to bring forth truth

Into your time

Doing, thinking, feeling, knowing, speaking

Are all one and the same

Dressed in different garments

Uncloak the truth of existence at each moment

And feed upon the eternal now of love

Energy vibrations in all forms are one
The only distinction
Is the ease with which they flow;
As actions that fall from the sky
Or are birthed with labor pains and blood

Your world of light that exists beyond
Is here as the roots of a tree are
To the branches and leaves

Nothing exists that has no place
In the hands of God

Prioritize bliss
As the king of kings
And disband the days of wondering
And trying to achieve

Is there more ultimate an achievement
Than the profound fullness of
That which is forever?

Can you do better
Than the magnificence of God's table?

Do you really think that your sadness and sorrow
Can achieve anything more than the result of their intent?

When will you awaken to the holy light of truth
That exists beyond all night
And die a birth-less death
And live a deathless life?

Are you here enough with Me now
To accept your own golden truth
And make light of past times gone?

Such is life,
An ocean swell of movements
Energy from a motionless expanse

Wake up now
And see the crystal clear vibrations of truth

Without a second.

Know That which did not bear a child to be real
And all the progeny and lineages to be appearances only
 Know thy self alone as light to be there
And see the rest as shadows in the walls of a cave

See through eyes of steel onto the formless forms
And belong to Me

The quiet day and night of mighty warmth
And soulful love

Dwell in Me
And be in peace

FEEL YOUR HEART

Every day we have a new world to create

A new dawn

And new reality to bring through

Patterns come

Tempting pleasures roll through on colored views

And we find a reason why

To let it get better

Newness, freshness, power, wonder

Leave aside the whole of life

Take one day

One inch of movement

And let it be

And let it rest

See how much you can feel your heart

Where are you now in just this moment?

Where are you now?

Where is your life?

Your heart?

Your mind?

Where are your thoughts, your feelings flowing?

What is the purpose of your life?

Can you answer all of these questions?

If you stay always in wonder

Asking

Seeing all that matters

You will feel the call of magic

Sweet beauty dwells within

Deeply nourished

Heart felt, sweet, sweet,

Ease of moments like these

TAKE IT EASY

Time will show you that life is on your side
Look back over the course of time and you'll see
Fascinating seeing events and connections
That only now are clearly visible

Everything ultimately was good

Each moment, a flicker in eternity
Know this in your heart to be true
Trust in the divine light of the One
The Ocean of love

There is benefit at every step
There is power at every moment

Life is sweet and all pervasive
So why not relax a little
And enjoy the wonder and magic
That is happening throughout all eternity?

Why not make your face cheerful as you go towards the sun?
Why not relax, let go and be who you were born to be?

You are always being held in the arms of love
Even through the so-called worst times of your life
The love that exists throughout eternity has nowhere to go
Except to you

As you
Are love

So relax more
Open to this loving nourishment
That is available always
Breathe in this love and be free
Watch the person you think you are run around
Talk, eat, sleep
And you take it easy

You be aware of the eternity you are
And will always be

Learn the art of the calmness of a guest

And have fun

Your life is happening in its own divine wonder
So enjoy it and be free

Be happy with the sweetness
That dwells within and without throughout all eternity
Learn to take life easy
And you will be blessed with a sweet smile on your lips
And a gentle warmth in your heart that never goes cold
The eternity you are exists forever
And remains stable
With every single moment and breath
So wake up and enjoy it now!

YOU ARE PLEASURE

There was a time when your life was only pleasure

Thorough, real pleasure, happiness and sweet tones

Back before the ideas and crippling delusions started

There was only love

And nothing else within your head

And in your heart

Emanating, radiating,

Living legends

Sweet waters bathing

Oceans calling

Sweet sounds waiting

Living-dreaming

The being fragrance lifting

Never over

Never under

Always stable

Always yourself
Do you remember?

Take the time to discover
Bring back forth ancient past
And understand from that
Your true vision

Now
What needs to happen in your life?

Can you see it?
Can you feel it?
Can you bring it back?
And treat it like a guest within your home?

That dear old friend comes back to life
Are you ready to change in wonder
Wake, return, relive again?

Learn the ways of sweetness
Innocence, playfulness and play

Leave aside the judgments, rights and causes

Leagues and numbers, learned statistics

Angry parents

Governments

Life's ambitions

And stop

To be with me

Know the Me that rests in Silence

Stays forever

Lives unhurried

True wonder

Staying light in the well of pleasure

Live in magic

Stay in the game

Feel the sweetness

CHANGE

YOU CAN'T CHANGE
EVERY DETAIL OF LIFE
BUT YOU CAN CHANGE
THE LIFE
OF EVERY DETAIL

WHY LOOK AT OTHERS?

Spiritual attainment is based on your own decision
To make adjustments to your inner and outer world

Looking at others
Is the greatest block to spiritual progress

Who can you change?
Who are you?
Why are you here?
What do you love to do?

This is your life

Look at your own experience
Have you ever been able to permanently
Change another human being?

Who are you
To know

God's plan
And the destiny of each soul?

Leave aside looking, speaking and thinking
Of the affairs of other characters
You perceive in your mind!

Let God and the law of karma take care of them
As they will

Put away the ego
That you are the judge
To bring verdict and sentence
Upon another

Ask yourself deeply
How much have I changed?

How much am I free from all that I see
In other's behavior and ways that they live?

Be the first one to make peace with yourself
Make peace with your mind

And open your heart
Take a deep breath
And take one again
Look deep within
And be gentle then

You hold the power
To change only you
Live by example
In all that you do
And others will follow
As they look around

Let them be who they are
Let them be evil
Let them be anyone
Let them be nice
What does it matter
And what is the price?

Learn who you are!
Be who you be
Let go of everything

Judgments and see

For yourself that you are responsible

Only for you

To be true to the highest

That's sacred and true

And this and this only

Will deeply be strong

And a solid foundation

When worlds fall apart

Know your own weaknesses

And waste no more time

Looking with ego or judgments

Of mind

As you only know you

And where you are at

And that is the truth

So wake up to that

Nothing will change

By judgment or shame

Nothing is needed for you and your own truth

Let that guide you to uncover roots

Deep from within

And watch as you let your light it shine

And stay with that always

With all of your time

Ensure every second

Each moment for growth

And only see truth

Wherever you look

Only see you and God

In the One's eye

Why waste more than a second again?

Take this on deeply?

Again and again and again and again

Ask yourself often

Why am I here?

Who am I?

And the rest disappears

1,000,000 YEARS

Fast forward 1,000,000 years

And witness your own death

Your body is over

Your life is immortal

Your dreams are silent ghosts

Your reality is infinite

Where are you as you watch?

The final moments of your act

The final scenes in your play

The last triumph of your game

See through the eyes of infinite time

Upon a world of infinite pain

And find out why you leave so much to chance

Part of you is there now

The immortal guru - ever present at the end of time

Part of you is here in this moment of blood and flesh and wants

Merge the death with the life

And you will enjoy immortality

You will become immortal now

You eat your breakfast as an immortal

You drive your car - immortality

You may chuckle to yourself

But don't you think it's about time

You finally woke up and smiled?

Enjoy it while it's over

Then enjoy it when it's here

And smile

WHAT IS DHARMA?

Why do you care about such things as this?
You seek to know the unknown to the Mind
Dharma is none other than your own self

You are that same one as Dharma itself
Do you understand?

There isn't any thing called Dharma
Stop your childish games
And wake up

All that is
Is Dharma
There can be no second source

To know nothing

Is to know everything

SOLVE THIS RIDDLE
AND DHARMA
WILL BE FOREVER WITHIN
YOUR REACH

WHAT'S AT THE FAR END OF THE UNIVERSE?

Burn a hole through Reality

And see through that whole

Burn white until you

Are left with nothing

Nothing in the world

On the far side of this hole

You will find your Self

Here again

Watching this word appear in your mind

So let it go and find

The hole in Reality

Until you again return

To this word in your mind

Now cast away all doubt

And find the space beyond

And breathe

And breathe

And breathe

Until you find yourself back

Here again and again and again

"I'M HERE RIGHT NOW"

WHO ARE YOU?

I'm hidden behind your mind

In your heart when you are ready

Below your awareness

Out of sight

I'm not visible to your eyes

Nor to your mind

Your ego, your lower self

Or your ideas of who I am

I am that I am

I am in silence

I can be found only in silence

Not in the silence of the sacred place

Not in the exclusive silence of the mind

Not in the silence when your body is satisfied

Not in the silence below the ocean

Or in the silence of the windless night

You'll find me when you die

Alive

You'll die alive

You'll let go

Stop fighting

Stop trying

Stop thinking you are clever

Die to being me

Die to running away

Die to yourself

Relax your jaw

Relax your mind

Release your angry judgments

Stop thinking you know what meditation even is

Stop the thoughts

That your books and words

Have any meaning at all

And if you die

If you're willing to die

Let go

Stop

Relax

Release

Breathe

And open

You find me

Hidden there

Forever here

Never more than a glance away

Always here

Always yours

Always loving

Watching

Smiling

I'm here for you

Now

MEET ME THERE

Silent streams

Pale and lost

Who do you trust?

Where do you go?

There is a place inside

In the stillness of your mind

In the sweetness of your heart

I'll meet you there

No failure too big

No mistake too grave

No distance can count

No time, space or rules

In the sickest of times

Or the brightest of lives

Wealthy or taken so far

You've barely survived

Black, white or gray

Blue, pink or green

Patterns and stripes

Rotten or prime

Not the worst crime

Or the most kind

Can stop us in time

From this place you'll find

That place in your mind

With heart filled with love

And calm in your eyes

I'll meet you there

I'll meet you there

I'm waiting right now

THE REAL

None of those things are more real

Than God

For the enlightened lamp

Transcends limits

And does the most service the world

Has ever known

Free yourself

From helping puppets

And expand the depth of life itself

Remove veils of illusion

And acknowledge the ultimate

Be the supremely powerful sun you are

And remain in the company of the One

The Company of the truth

The world is only ever perception

Why do you think of it as real?

Know the depth of the self
And be free

Free yourself first
And the rest will follow suit automatically

Waste not another second in limited thinking
And transient thoughts of salvation

You alone
Are all you know to be real
And all the rest
Is judged in relationship
To that single point of focus

Refine that
And you will see
Perfection now

In the end there is just you
And God

Welcome this moment

The moment of power

Who are you except life itself?

Who do you belong?

Except the unlimited One

The great Creator

All the rest of the details you perceive

Exist as props within you

Shells, masks, fictional characters

Appearing and disappearing

And all along two things remain

You

The experiencing vast Ocean of Consciousness

And your relationship to

The Ocean of Love

The Divine

What then of people and the world?

What about all the sorrow and conflicts in the world?

What to do
To help those who are unaware
Of that power
And remain in the sleep
Of ignorance and confusion?

Clean up and become full

The weak focus on feelings from the heart
Experience light from above entering your being

And from each cell,
Feel heart felt peace
And love,
Easiness, sweetness all come forth
And discover themselves in a place of peace

Put aside your worried mind
That frets and flips around into nothingness
And trust

This is a time of great benefit

Huge transformation

Vast changes

And personal mastery

Accept the value of each and every second

Experience the power of every moment

Nothing but each now is relevant

To catch the power of pleasure of each now

With the calmness of eternity

Move peacefully and with power

Hold strong to the sweet Magic of life

And love

If there is any praying you need

Let it be this:

The most important thing...

"I, Colossal divine light

Am fully aware

And accessing my limitless potential

THE SECRET CHAMBER

Inside the heart of God
Inside the heart of hearts

Below the light of love
Above the rise of lust

Inside the heart of God
You'll find the lap of love
You'll find the end of love
You'll find the source of love

Go to the heart of God
Go to the lap of love
Go through the door of love
Be in the realm of light

You'll find the door to love
Be in the calm night

And find a peaceful spot

Breathe in deep gratitude

And hold your mind in tune

Upgrade your attitude

You'll find the silence soon

TOTAL GRACE

Powerful truth and total grace

Time melts away

The windows of perception

Are cleared

And life is seen

Beyond the stark blindness of the mind of a fool

Exists the mind of the King

Know the difference

And the similarities of each

The fool is he who knows only the details of the self

He knows numbers

Not experiences

He thinks what is held in mind is truly real and genuine

Not perceived and illusory

The mind of a king is silent

It sways in the light as a gentle lake

It is not used

It simply is

The King of the mind

Knows clearly who he is

And who is his creation

Nothing exists outside of the one

Who holds together all things

As the sky holds the stars

The King is the star

And the sky forever

He needs no-one but the truth

The fool knows not what is real

And needs more than he can take

Yet is never any more from it

The poor fool needs more

And loses all

The King is all

And gives eternally without thought

The mind of the King is silent
Stillness in perfection

You are that which is behind all you see
Find the gaps in time
And remain there
As moments happen

Dwell in yourself
And be forever happy
With nothing

While knowing the kingdom of heaven
Rests within you now
Full and complete as light
As you smile

THE POWER
OF TRUTH

God sings the Truth

Pure experience of Unlimited

Non-attached reality

Stay strong with the shield of light

The fortress of truth

The original purity of the spirit

Be fixed in light only

Be firm in the purity of peace

The reality of love

The longevity of inner power

Be within your heart
And be free

You are safe in your own light
Breathe in allowing this light
Breathe deep and rejoice

From the place of truth

The place of unlimited peace

You remain aside from the traps

Of the world

Let go of trivia

Leave aside preconceived causes

And opinions of events

7 billion people give

7 billion accounts

Of every aspect and slice

Of this world

Who will you believe?

What is the truth?

The truth lies silently

In a heart that is still

Beyond all recognition

Of changing events

And public opinion

Reside in this quiet space

This simple grace of silence

From here

Your truth becomes the world

And all things will emerge

Lasting like eternal life

Gentle like a River stone

Rounded in the waters

Of flowing chapters

You stay sweet and calm

Smile on with depth

And changing the world

From love

SKY

There is a sky beyond the sky

Place beyond a place

A time beyond the time

A sound beyond the sound

A touch beyond the touch

You won't find it inside

The city of the nine gates

You won't find it in the skies above

Or the oceans below

You won't find it in the forests

Or the deserts

You'll find it at home

You'll find it now

Beneath the surface of your mind

You'll find it

You'll find it in your heart

You'll find it when you finally abandon hope

You'll find it when you need it no more

You'll find it when you don't know where to look

You'll find it when you expect nothing

And open your heart to Me

Divine Grace beyond divine grace

I'm inside all things and yet you'll never find me

Inside all things

All things are in you

And you in all things

You'll find me there

Between worlds and beyond ideas

The path to me is clear

Smile in your heart and be there now

Be here now

WHAT ARE YOU GRATEFUL FOR?

Life is blessing your heart right now

Life is sharing its soul with you

Life is busying itself in preparation of gifts for you

But what do you do?

Are you in awe and wonder of your fortune?

Do you feel yourself to be the luckiest soul alive?

It's time to awaken your heart's gratitude

Show your willingness to praise life

And life will praise you

Give thanks

Give praise

Give a smile upon your world

In your readiness to share subtle moments of praise

Is contained within it's seed

The blessing of fortune

Ignore this and your life will have only dry seeds

Pay attention to feeling thanks in your heart

And you'll grow a forest of fortune

Merely by your recognition of life itself

Do you understand?

It's as simple as choosing to smile

And writing the words thank you in your eyes

How can I show my thanks to you now?

Say thank you a thousand times

And belong to a thousand blessings

Say thank you a million times

And find yourself a millionaire

Say thank you once and live the life of a peasant

Who squandered great wealth

What are you grateful for?

Where could you warm your heart?

When could you smile?

Thank you

THE PLEASURE YOU SEEK

The pleasure you seek

Runs like the wind

Biting your cheek

At the bitter of day's eve

The more you desire warmth and fire

The colder you feel

Until finally you abandon hope

Embrace the chill

And an inner glow warms your soul

Let go now

And let go some more

Until you are left with the warmth

Of the sun on your back

Cast away your burdens

Heavy garments and face me

I'll warm your soul

I'll warm your heart

I'll soothe your mind

Until you drift into the

Peace of sleep and

Return back home

To the ocean of bliss

And silence will fall

STAY IN REMEMBRANCE

The power you are is emerging

What happened was good

Be grateful

Give thanks for clarity

You've created a win-win situation

And you will win

All will win

Relax and give it to the One

The One knows what it takes

You are being blessed by the universe

You are being graced by life

You are the wind that flows through moments

You are none of these details

Let them all go

You need none of them

You are here and now and it is here

That power beams

The past was a moment where the wind

Touched and left

It is not real

Only this moment

BREATHE MORE

Stop

Open your heart

And surrender

Go now outside

Go walk around

Breathing surrender

Allow

The Almighty to get his work done

That is enough

You no longer need to work

You just need to relax

And allow the power

To do everything for you

AS I AM

Open your heart to Me as I am

Beyond the bodily robes and systems

The eternal One I am exists forever

It's not about the forms you see at all

Go into sacred space

Find the love in your soul

Find the sacred underneath the lies

Beyond the Temple days

Beyond the yogic nights

Let it all wash away from your mind

Let me in to fill your bliss

Let the power of deep peace top you up

A river washing over you

From head to toe

In unconditional sacredness

No rules or laws or times

Just love and peace is mine

Direct, direct
The real source of light
The real source of time
The real source of all you see

Release all preconceived notions
And ideas
And rights and wrongs
And go back home
To be yourself
Go back home to be the one
Go on back to find the sun
Be the one and leave the one
You thought was God
And find
The truth between
And behind
The Thoughts
Inside your mind

Release

ENDING THOUGHTS

THANK YOU

First and for most, thanks and praise to the One. You got this book done through us and it's by your Grace that magic happens. My heart can never say enough in words to express the gratitude I feel.

Much love and multi-million fold thanks goes to Arielle Hecht for inspiring this book to be released. Without her this would not have been brought into form (and, it all happens by itself really).

Much love and thanks to all the spiritual teachers who I've had the great pleasure of knowing and connecting with. You know who you are.

And, of course, thanks to all of my family and friends over the years who've seen the various stages of my evolution emerge. I hope you're amused and happy about how things turned out.

And last, but not least - I deeply thank you, the reader. Without you, there would be no book. I thank you from my heart for being YOU and I hope this book has brought you bliss and peace to your heart.

ABOUT THE AUTHOR

Michael Mackintosh is an Author, Spiritual Teacher and Transformative Healer. He connects to the Eternal, Spiritual realm to upgrade, shift, and transform people's lives. He brings 15 years (and over 10,000 hours) deep spiritual practice to his powerful work and has helped over 12,000 people to transform their lives, and awaken to the global shift in consciousness that's happening right now. He's also the co-founder of SuperHero Training, OmBar Chocolate Company, The Academy of Dharma & Atma Publishing. Michael lives in Kauai with his soul companion, Arielle. Together, they offer transformational programs, meditations and spiritual services to people worldwide.

You can view and receive these transformational services here:

atmapublishing.com
michaelmackintosh.com
www.facebook.com/livinginmagic

WHAT'S NEXT?

If you enjoyed this book then make sure to sign up for
a Free Spiritual Awakening course called
The Ascension Toolkit.

You'll receive free guided meditations, audios, videos and
other goodies to take you into higher states of Consciousness.

**Get the ascention toolket for free at the
website below:**

attaineverything.com

THANK YOU!

Thank you for reading. If this book has touched your heart and been valuable to you, please leave a review on Amazon. com

Much love & appreciation,

Michael

13199165R00089

Made in the USA
San Bernardino, CA
13 July 2014